EXCEL
MACROS

A Step-by-Step Guide to Learn and Master Excel Macros

TABLE OF CONTENTS

Introduction

Congratulations on purchasing *Excel Macros: A Step-by-Step Guide to Learn and Master Excel Macros*, and thank you for doing so.

Even though Excel comes with hundreds of built-in spreadsheet functions, there are times when you want to customize your functions. There is no better way to do so than to create your own functions using Excel macros.

With Excel macros, you have the ability to add your own macros to the Excel menu function and use them as you would the built-in functions any time. A macro is simply a snippet of computer code written in Excel form using the Visual Basic language.

Have you ever thought about how much time you spend on Excel completing small, repetitive tasks? Whether you have or haven't, you must have realized that frequent tasks such as inserting standard text and formatting take up a lot of time. No matter your level of practice in doing these tasks, the 3-4 minutes you spend daily to insert your company details in all Excel Worksheets before you can send them to your clients adds up every day.

In most cases, investing a lot of time in these small repetitive tasks doesn't produce much value. In fact, these are examples of efforts which have little impact on the overall output. By reading this book, you are going to learn how you can automate those small tasks using one of the most powerful Excel features.

Macro, in general, is a complicated topic. This means that if you want to become a pro in programming, you must be ready to learn and master Visual Basic language. This book will help you get started on becoming an advanced programmer in VBA.

There are plenty of books on this subject on the market, so thanks again for choosing this one! Every effort was made to ensure it is full of as much useful information as possible. Please enjoy!

Chapter 1

Getting Started with Excel Macros

Dear Reader,

The end of this chapter should see you well-informed about the basics of Excel Macros. In addition, you should be able to know what they are and why they are important. Let's get started, shall we?

Defining Excel Macro

Because you are just getting started with Excel Macro, we will not go into too much detail this early on. For now, you should just know that Macro is one of the most popular software among the numerous Windows applications. A lot of these said applications come with the Macro software built-in. In this book, we shall be covering how to use it in Excel.

Excel Macro gives users the ability to carry out numerous operations with just a click of the button or by simply changing the value of a cell. Macro will help you perform your daily tasks in the most efficient and interesting way. When we look at it based on productivity, we can say that it lends itself to productivity because it helps reduce a lot of the repetitive work that are usually done manually. Aside from that, it helps one perform operations faster. In fact, if you have tasks which need to be done frequently, Excel Macro is the best tool for you to use.

Can we say that Macro is a programming language?

At this point, the answer is in the affirmative: macro is not so different from Visual Basic. For the moment, you don't have to worry about the history of this language. Let's jump straight into the reasons why you need Excel Macros to make your work and daily life easier.

Why Create Excel Macro?

Many students find macros as something difficult and daunting. Once you understand and master the basics, however, you will find it to be one of the best software to enhance productivity. Here are a few reasons why you should aim to create Excel Macros.

1. Excel is your home

If you are one of those people who like to master quick tips, perhaps you consider Excel as your home. You should consider having keyboard shortcuts that can help you perform multiple tasks instead of only one. For instance, the delete key will only clear individual cell contents but not the comments and formatting. However, if you choose to apply a macro, it will help you delete all cell contents and formatting.

2. You frequently import text files

If you would like to boost the rate of importing a single text file, macros could be the way to go, allowing you to accomplish such a task in just a few minutes. Note, however, that if you want to import various text files at any one time, the macro will take longer to create.

3. You use an assistant

You might be fast when it comes to preparing a new month's sheet or product sheet with the correct headings, but what if you find a way these tasks could be done at no cost to you in terms of time? There's no need to be a master in VBA to create a macro that can automate different kinds of processes. You can simply use a recorder which will retain your keystrokes and convert them into a macro.

4. You want to safeguard information

One great thing about Excel is that it provides security for your formulas, files, and sheets. However, when you want to remove and reapply that security, it might take some time. A macro is the best remedy to use in this case. It will automatically perform the task faster and more accurately.

5. You want to merge information

If you are working with a large dataset and want to combine specific information, it would be tiresome to do it manually. But macros can quickly copy the range into a new data sheet or create an email attachment. The only thing which you must know before using a macro is that data merged by a macro is more advanced.

Recording a Macro

Where is the Excel Macro found in Excel?

If you are a beginner, you may be asking yourself what are "Macro" and "VBA" in the first place. Here is a crucial point: you don't need to worry about those two terms. I will suggest that you view the two terms as the same thing for now.

In this section, we shall be using MS Excel. We will record and write our first macro based on the requirements at hand. Therefore, we begin by explaining how to record a macro.

Macro Recording Basics

When it comes to recording a macro, the first thing to do is to search for the Macro Recorder at the Developer tab. However, in Excel, this tab is hidden, meaning you might not be able to see it quickly. Before you use the VBA macros, the Developer tab has to be accessible. To make the tab accessible, follow the steps below.

1. Select Excel Office Options.

2. An Excel dialog box will show up with options for you to select; pick the option, Customize Ribbon.

3. Check the mark near the Developer in the list box.

4. Finally, click OK and return to Excel.

It is important for the Developer tab to be visible in the Excel Ribbon. It will help you start recording a macro by just selecting the option Record Macro on the tab.

Below, we look at the Record Macro dialog box and describe its parts in detail:

Macro Name: It is important that you assign a name to your macro because Excel will give it a default name otherwise. The macro name should describe what it is going to perform.

Shortcut Key: Each macro must have an event that will take place for it to run. This event can include a press of a button or the opening of a Workbook. Once you assign the shortcut key to the macro and you press the key combinations, Excel Macro will start. Note, though, that this field is optional.

Store Macro In: A macro that is stored here means that it has an active Excel file. Therefore, if you open a specific Workbook, you can run the macro.

Description: This field is optional, but it can still be very useful when you have multiple macros in the spreadsheet. In addition, this field allows you to describe the macro to the user in greater detail.

Once the Record Macro dialog box shows up, the steps below will help you create a macro you can use to enter your name into a Worksheet.

1. First, specify the name of your macro. Don't go with the default name.

2. Next, allocate a unique shortcut key, such as Ctrl + Shift + N, to the macro.

3. Select OK and exit the dialog box before you start recording.

4. Click any cell in the Worksheet. Type your name and hit enter.

5. Finally, select Developer —> Code —> Stop Recording.

Reviewing the Macro

Youcan find the macro you created even in a new module. To look at the associated code, activate the Visual Basic Editor. There are two ways to activate the VB Editor.

1. Press Alt + F11.

2. Select Developer —> Code —> Visual Basic.

The project window of the VB Editor has a list of open Workbooks as well as add-ins. This list appears in the form of a tree that one can expand. The previous code you recorded is kept in the module of the available Workbook. Thus, if you double-click the module, the code will show up in the window. The macro should resemble what is shown below:

```
Sub MyName()
'
' MyName Macro
'
' Keyboard Shortcut: Ctrl+Shift+N
'
    ActiveCell.FormulaR1C1 = "Michael Alexander"
End Sub
```

You could see that the macro we have just recorded is a sub procedure. You should be able to see a few inserted comments by the application; these show up at the top of the procedure. Comments start with an apostrophe, but it is not necessary. We can delete the comments, leaving us with one VBA statement.

Macro Testing

Recall that before we recorded our first macro, we assigned it to the Ctrl + Shift + N combination keys. Now, testing this macro would entail returning to Excel. To do so, below are the steps one can follow:

1. Press Alt + F11.

2. Select the button View Microsoft Excel which can be found in the VB Editor toolbar.

Once that is open, activating the Worksheet comes next. This can be performed on the Workbook with the VBA module or on a different type of Workbook altogether. Click on a cell and use the command Ctrl + Shift + N. This will instantly enter your name in the cell.

Comparison of Absolute and Relative Macro Recording

So far, you've learned about the basics of Macro Recorder interface. It is now a good time for us to dig deeper and start recording macros in earnest. Before we do, it is important to understand the two models of recording in Excel. The first one is the absolute reference, and the other one is the relative reference.

Macro recording using absolute references

The absolute reference is the default mode for Excel. We refer to a cell reference as absolute if it can't automatically adjust when we paste a formula to a new cell location.

Macro recording using relative references

When talking about relative reference in Excel macros, we refer to how the reference automatically adjusts when it's moved or copied from one cell or column to another. This requires you to be careful in the way you apply active cell choice while you run and record the relative reference macro.

Other macro recording terms

Up to this point, you must be familiar with recording your Excel Macros. We'll now look at some other important terms which you must be aware of before handling macros.

File Extensions

Let's begin discussing the Excel 2007, as this contains unique file extensions for Workbooks that have macros. You will notice that for the 2010 Excel versions, Workbooks have a standard file extension which ends with .xlsx. In other words, .xlsx extensions don't contain macros. Therefore, having a Workbook that contains macro saved with the following extension will be removed automatically. You will receive an Excel warning that macros will be disabled when you save the Workbook as an .xlsx file.

However, if you are not ready to lose your macros, save it as an Excel Macro-Enabled Workbook. The extension .xlsx for Workbooks is considered safe. On the other hand, Workbooks with the .xlsm extension are considered as a potential threat.

Recording a Macro in Excel

Use the steps outlined in this section to record macros in Excel.

Step 1: Open an Excel Workbook.

Step 2: Navigate to the Developer tab.

Step 3: Find the Record Macro button.

Step 4: If you are using Excel 2007 or 2010, you need to go at the bottom of the Excel; look in the left side and find the button shown below, encased in a red rectangle.

Step5: Click the Record Macro button found in the previous picture.

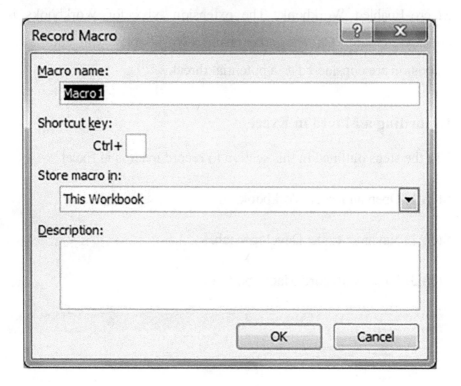

Step 6: If you look at the dialog box shown above, you'll see it has places for you to type the name of the macro. If you want, you can write the name of the shortcut key you would want to use to run the recorded macro. That way, any time you press on that specific macro key, it will run by default.

Step 7: The choice is yours on whether to pick a location to store the macro and/or write a description about the macro.

Step 8: Once you are done filling the fields in the dialog box, click OK and perform a few operations on the Excel sheet. This could include cell formatting or sorting values.

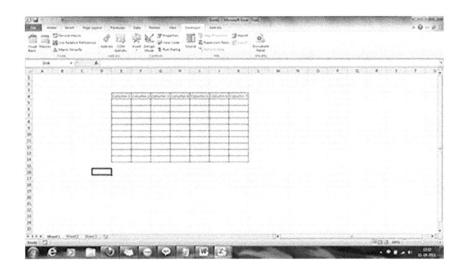

Step 9: If you want to look at your recorded macro, just right-click the sheet name and then go to View Code.

Step 10: Navigate to the left-hand side panel and click it to expand the module.

Step 11: You will see an already created module labeled "Module 1." Click on that module.

Step 12: You will be able to see the code recorded together with the assigned Macro name.

Running the Macro by Pressing the Play Button

There are two ways to run the recorded macro. The first one is by selecting the run button, and the second one is by using the key combination Alt + F8.

In this particular macro, I deleted the formatting done when it was recorded. Therefore, running the macro will make the formatting details show up in the sheet. That sounds magical, doesn't it? Now, it's time to see how you can run the macro by using the run button in the VBA IDE. The image below is of a clean Excel sheet.

Step 1: Navigate to the screen code that has VBA. The Workbook screen does not display the play button.

Step 2: Hover the mouse's pointer near the particular macro you wish to test.

Step 3: Select the Play or Run button, as indicated by the red box in the following image.

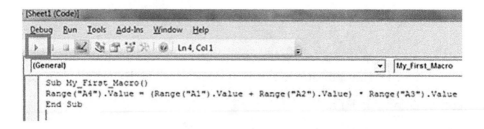

Congratulations on running your first recorded macro! You can look at the image below and compare it with yours.

14

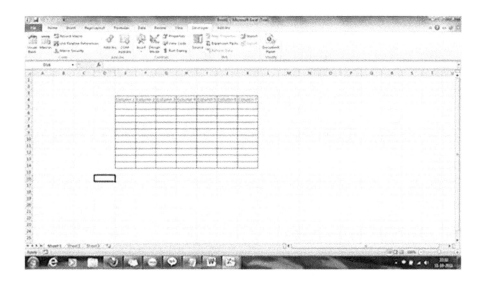

Note

Let's say you failed to position your mouse's cursor around the VBA code that you want to run; the pop-up list below containing all the macros in the Workbook will show up for you to select the correct one.

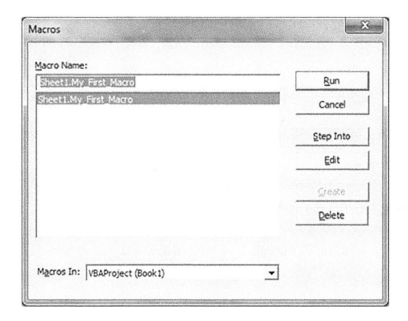

Now that you're getting the hang of things let's find out how you can run the macro without the need to jump to the VBE screen. If you aren't comfortable with the previous method of running the macro, there is another way where you can run it while in the Worksheet screen. Try and use the steps below as well to create and run your macro.

Step 1: Use the Alt + F8 shortcut key. A pop-up screen like the one indicated below will show up.

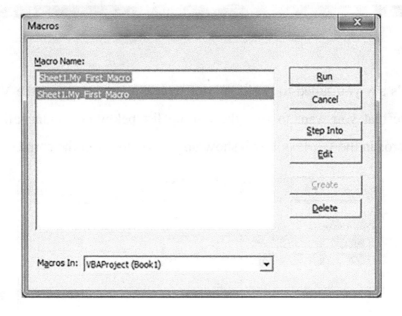

Step 2: A drop-down list will show up; choose your macro.

Step 3: Run the macro by clicking Run.

And you're done! You can now record and play macro in the Excel Workbook.

Chapter 2

Security in Excel Macros

Excel 2010 Macro Security

When Microsoft released Excel 2010, it came with an interesting feature which had new settings on the security model. The most popular update was on the trusted document. This is a document which you have approved to be safe through macros permission.

In Excel 2010, when you open a Workbook which has macros, you will see a yellow message that pops up below the Ribbon to indicate that macros are disabled. Now, clicking on Enable would make it a trusted document. You will no longer be constantly required to enable the content whenever you open the PC.

The concept applied here is simple: once you trust a document through enabling macros, there is no need to enable macros every time you open the document again. This means that Excel records the first time you gave permission and prevents additional messages requesting you to enable the macros the next time you open the Workbook.

This is a great thing because it saves one from the constant annoying messages concerning the macros. No more worries that your macros will fail because macros are disabled!

Trusted Locations

In case you are worried about macros messages showing up, you should decide to create a trusted location. This refers to a specific directory where only trusted workbooks can be considered safe to be kept. This type of location provides one with the use of a macro-enabled Workbook which has no security settings enforced. The only condition is that you must have the Workbook in this location. The steps to create a trusted location are shown below:

1. Choose the Macro Security button located at the Developer tab.

2. Select the button labeled Trusted Location. A Trusted Location menu would appear.

3. Choose the Add New Location button from the list that shows up.

4. Select Browse to look for the directory that you want to consider a trusted location.

Once you have chosen a trusted location, whichever Excel file you open from that location will have macros already enabled.

Storing Macros in the Personal Macro Workbook

A lot of macros created by users are meant to be used on one particular Workbook, but there are some macros that you can use on multiple different works. The Personal Macro Workbook is where these types of macros need to be stored. This means you will always have access to them any time they're needed. This kind of Workbook will be available when you open the Excel program.

18

To record a macro, it is important that you first select a Personal Macro Workbook in the dialog box. You can find that option in the Macro's drop-down menu. Storing Macros in the Personal Macro Workbook can save time whenever you want to use a Workbook. When you want to exit, a pop-up message will show up to request whether you want to save the changes.

Allocating a Button to a Macro

When you have a macro set up, you need to have an easy and clear way to run each one. A typical button should create an effective and easy user interface. Excel has a set of form controls which could help one create different user interfaces on the spreadsheets. Various types of form controls exist, including buttons and scrollbars.

The basic concept on how to use a form control is straightforward. On the spreadsheet, place the form control in position and assign it a recorded macro. Once you have a macro allocated to a control, you can execute the macro by clicking the control.

Chapter 3

Send Email in Excel Macros

E mails are an important element in any program because they help save the time it would take to go to the email applications. Aside from that, it helps enhance the functionality of the program.

There are a lot of good reasons why you need to automate sending emails inside Microsoft Office Products such as Excel or Word. One reason is that you might want to get a notification when there are updates that happen in the spreadsheets you are working on. You might also need to send a report on the existing data in the spreadsheets.

When you want to be able to send emails from Excel, you need to know some techniques to help you automate the process.

Collaboration Data Objects

This is a messaging component present in Windows and other OS generations. This component already comes with the VBA installation in the Microsoft Excel. This component helps make sending emails in Windows Excel very easy.

Create VBA Macro

The first thing to do is to navigate to the Excel Developer tab, click on Insert, and choose a command button. Move on and create a macro. Once Excel opens the VBA editor, you will be required to add a reference to the CDO library. To do this, go to Tools —> References located in the editor. Go through the list until you can find Microsoft CDO for Windows. Highlight the checkbox before you click OK.

Set Up CDO

At this point, you are good to go and can send emails from Microsoft Excel. To achieve this, create the mail objects and fill all the fields relevant to send the email. Make sure that the TO and FROM fields are filled properly.

Configure CDO to Work with an External SMTP

The next part of the code is to configure CDO to operate with an external SMTP server.

Finalize CDO setup

Once you have connected the SMTP server for sending emails, the next thing to do is to complete all the fields for the CDO_Mail object and specify the Send command. Once you have done this, you will be ready to go. With CDO, you will not see any pop-up boxes like when you are using Outlook Mail object. CDO will combine the email and make use of the SMTP server connection details to trigger the message.

Chapter 4

Beginning Programs with VBA

In this chapter, we are going to learn some basic concepts of programming using VBA.

Data Types, Variables, and Constants

As this text aims to deal with spreadsheet applications, we shall introduce the concept of variables by asking a few questions.

1. What are some of the values that one can enter into a spreadsheet cell?

2. What are the ways you can use these values?

If you have ever used a spreadsheet to manage your data, you are already capable of entering text and numbers into Excel spreadsheet cells. In addition, you might already be capable of changing the format of a spreadsheet cell. Perhaps you can format a number such that the values can show up on the right side of a decimal point, or perhaps you can format numbers so that they appear as a percentage or currency. You might know how to have the texts automatically convert into time or date. Furthermore, you can perhaps change the content of a spreadsheet any time you want.

22

Typically, cells in a spreadsheet represent a temporary storage location where you can store text and numbers in different formats. This is similar to how a variable is described in any programming language. Variables are used in programming for temporary data storage. This means that the data you enter are converted into variables and are stored as such to later be used in the program.

Declaring variables

Whenever you declare a variable, you make the program reserve a space in its memory to be used later. Variables are declared by using the **Dim** statement. Below is an example:

Dim myClass As Integer

In the above example, the name of the variable is myVar. It is important to note that the name must start with an alphabetic character, but it should not be more than 255 characters nor have spaces. When declaring a variable, avoid the use of unusual characters or punctuation marks when giving it a name. This is because, aside from the underscore character, these are not permitted. The underscore is used to delineate multiple words that exist in a single variable name. When doing variable declaration, avoid using reserved keywords of the VBA language and repeating variable names in the same scope. Make sure that the name of the variable resembles something related to the task it should perform.

Object and Standard Modules

These procedures and declarations come in a set and are all related. Every module contains a separate window in the VBA IDE. In addition, it will contain a separate behavior based on the variable declarations. Modules basically carry all event procedures related to the Worksheet. For object modules, it might have programmer-defined procedures. Every Worksheet will contain a different window code just like the Workbook.

A modularized code is very useful when you want to break complex programming problem into smaller problems and develop a solution for each of them. This process is very important when you want to create software applications.

The Scope of a Variable

When we talk about scope in the context of a variable, we refer to the time when a variable is present in a given section of the program. A variable present in a given scope can not only be accessed but also be further influenced. A variable that is out of scope, on the other hand, is not accessible to the program.

Variables whose declaration falls within a procedural code block is referred to as a procedural level variable. A procedural level program appears only in the presence of program execution inside the procedure where variables were declared. In the figure below, the variable myVar4 is present in the program when we have the Activate () event running on the Worksheet.

When this program execution reaches the End Sub, the variable is cleared from memory. This means it will not be in the scope anymore.

```
Private Sub Worksheet_Activate()
Static myVar4 As Integer
myVar4 = myVar4 + 1
End Sub
```

If you want to make your variable a module level variable, declare it outside the procedure using a Dim statement. The module level variable scope relies on the keyword type that has been applied in the declaration. The keyword declared with these variables include Private, Dim, and Public.

Data Types

The function of data types is to specify the type of value which can be kept in the memory that is set aside for a given variable. Similar to spreadsheet cells, there are many kinds of data types.

Numerical Data Types

Examples of numerical data types include double, integer, long, and single. A variable that has been declared as a long data type or integer can store non-fractional values or whole numbers in a given range. When you want a variable to store a floating point or fractional value, you should apply double or single data types.

Make sure that you check the value assigned to the number. This is because a very big value will cause your program to crash. Again, you should pay attention that you don't mix other data types with numerical data types. This might cause you to fail to get the correct results.

Other Data Types

Other data types include Boolean, Variant, and String.

Constants

In programming languages exists constants. The role of a constant is to help one assign a meaningful name to a string or number, improving the readability of the code. There are a lot of mathematical constants, and that makes it sensible to use the constant data type. You use a constant string in situations that require you to frequently use a given spreadsheet label. We declare constants with the Const keyword. This has been illustrated below:

```
Const PI = 3.14159
Dim circumference As Single
Dim diameter As Single
diameter = 20.34|
circumference = PI* diameter
```

You declare and initialize a constant in the same line. What is vital to note is that once we initialize a constant with a value, it remains that way until we change it. This makes it a good move to use a constant in cases where you have to use the same value in the entire program. Constants' names are defined in capital letters.

Using VBA to Input and Output

There are situations that arise while using Excel spreadsheet wherein you require something more dynamic than a spreadsheet cell. In this situation, the easiest way you can collect user input and send the output is through the InputBox () and MsgBox (). The same way Excel has numerous functions that you can use as spreadsheet formulas, VBA has multiple functions designed to help a programmer. In addition, these functions require one or two more parameters so that it can return one or more values.

Gathering User Input with InputBox ()

In case you are faced with a situation where you want to request a user for some input and at the same time prompt a response before program execution proceeds, this is the right function to apply. This function will launch a dialog screen that the user has to address before the execution of a program can resume.

```
InputBox(prompt [,title] [,default] [,xpos] [,ypos] [,helpfile, context])
```

Gathering User Output with MsgBox ()

This function will display a message to the user through a message box. The message box is one of the best ways you can notify the user when a problem happens. It can also be used to throw a question that has a yes/no response to the user. Below is the syntax of a MsgBox ().

```
MsgBox(prompt[, buttons] [, title] [, helpfile, context])
```

Manipulating Strings Using VBA Functions

Like most functions, you have to pass at least one or more parameters to the string functions. All these functions should return a value. Below is an example of a syntax:

```
myVar = FunctionName(parameter list)
```

Chapter 5

Procedure and Conditions

This chapter will help you look at procedures and conditions so that you can determine the basic tools that you can work with VBA.

VBA Procedures

We looked at modules in brief in a previous chapter. If you can still recall, we defined it as a set of declarations and procedures that are related. What we didn't say is that a module has its unique window in the VBA code editor. Procedures in programming can be created inside each of the above window modules. Below, we look at various procedures which you can apply in VBA.

Event Procedures

Some of the procedures in VBA include Click () and SelectionChange (). VBA defines the above procedures so that it is not possible to change the existing object or name in the Excel where the procedure is found. In addition, you cannot change the conditions where the procedure is activated. Normally, multiple events are linked with every Excel object in a Workbook or Worksheet. To define event procedures, you need to use the Sub keyword as shown below:

```
Private Sub Worksheet_Activate()
'Event procedure code is listed here.
End Sub
```

In the above figure, the name of the procedure is *Worksheet_Activate ()* even though most people simply call it Activate (). As you can see in the above procedure, we haven't passed any parameters to it. This procedure becomes functional when we activate the Worksheet that it has been linked to. The procedure ends at the lines End Sub. Still, you can use the Exit Sub statement in the procedure code to end the procedure.

Parameters that Have Event Procedures

Parameters refer to a collection of variables used by the event procedures. The parameter values which exist in the event procedure carry information that is associated with the event. We use a comma to separate variables as well as declared variable data types. The VBA language defines all the parameters in the event procedure plus the number of parameters, data types, and method in which it has been passed. While you will still be able to make some changes to the variable names in the parameter list, this is never recommended.

Private, Public, and Procedure Scope

This is not the first time for you to come across the keywords Private and Public. We use these keywords to define procedures, and they serve the same purpose as when they are applied to declaring variables. We use Private and Public to set the scope of a procedure.

As the name suggests, Public keyword allows the procedure to be accessible by other procedures in the project module. On the other hand, the Private keyword is slightly different. This keyword only makes procedures accessible in a given module but prevents its visibility from the rest of other procedures defined. As you can see, it operates the same way a variable scope does. In VBA language, we have Private and Public keywords optional. However, they can be useful in predefined event procedures. In case we remove the Private or Public keyword, the procedure becomes the default.

Tip

When creating general declarations in a module, learn how to apply the Option Private statement so that you can ensure public modules remain visible in the project. If you want to have a reusable procedure, you should remove the Private option.

Sub Procedures

You know that virtually all procedures are subs. Sub is the short form for Subroutine. We use this term to refer to those procedures which have been designed for the programmer's use. A sub procedure's basic declaration is not different from that of an event procedure. This procedure is defined using the Private or Public keywords before it is followed with a Sub keyword, the name of the procedure, and finally the parameter. We end the subprocedures with the statement End Sub. Below is the syntax:

```
Private Sub myProcedure(parameter list)
'Sub procedure code is listed here.
End Sub
```

It is easy to get confused between procedures and sub procedures. Below, we provide you with how the subprocedure is different:

- Both the variable name and procedure name are defined in the parameter list.

- The programmer will decide the number of variables contained in the parameter list.

- The process of execution starts when it is called from different sections of the program.

- Subprocedures can be placed both in standard and object modules.

Tip

When you write procedures, make sure that you aim to keep them short. You will come to realize that longer procedures become difficult for one to read, and the same is true when it comes to fixing errors that may arise. As a general rule, let your procedures remain within a length where they can be visible in the computer screen.

ByVal and ByRef

These two are keywords used in VBA programming. The ByVal keyword creates a copy of the stored variable. This means that when there is a modification of the created copy, it will not interfere with the original variable.

On the other hand, when we look at ByRef, it is a way for us to pass a variable to another procedure by referencing it. This method of variable passage involves passing the original variable to the procedure. This is not like ByVal where we pass a copy and, therefore, whenever we make any modification to a variable passed by reference, that change becomes permanent.

The most important thing that you need to remember is that we use pass by reference when you want to make some changes to the original variable value. However, in situations where you want to change the variable but still retain the initial value, pass by value is applied.

Function Procedures

These procedures are not different to other procedures apart from just one distinct feature, and that is, they return a value to the procedure that called it. If you have used a few of the basic Excel functions before, then you know how they work. In most cases, we pass one or more values to a function and, in turn, the function must return at least one value.

Creating Personal VBA Functions

To create a function procedure in VBA, use the syntax below:

```
Private/Public Function FunctionName(paramter list) as type
'Function procedure code is listed here
FunctionName = Return value
End Function
```

If you are keen, you should realize that this is similar to the way you define a procedure. It is important that when you create a function procedure, you include Private and Public to specify the scope of the function. The clearest difference is that we have the Function keyword replacing Sub. Furthermore, your function procedure should have a return type. This represents the value which the program will send to the calling procedure. Now, when you fail to define the data type, the return type of the function will be variant.

Tip

Use Exit Function and Exit Sub when you want to switch the program back to the procedure which called it prior to the whole code in the procedure run. Don't forget that we call a function from expressions that would essentially insert a literal or a variable.

Chapter 6

Basic Excel Objects

This chapter will talk you through some of the VBA-Excel programming concepts.

VBA Object-Oriented Programming

If it is your first time learning about VBA programming, chances are it's also your first time to hear about object-oriented programming. Don't get scared if this is so. VBA is not an OO programming language. There exist certain features which exclude VBA from being considered an object-oriented programming language, but you will still find some common concepts common to both.

In most cases, VBA and object-oriented language share similarity based on the objects and tools used to change the objects. The tools consist of events, methods, and properties. In other languages, these tools have different names, but they are essentially the same things.

Define Objects

We shall not be abstract in the definition of an object. Essentially, it's the easiest thing for anyone to understand. You should view objects as independent computer programs that have a customized function present for frequent use in programs. The best feature of objects is that they are dynamic; i.e., one can make changes in code.

In the English language, we consider objects as nouns. In programming language, meanwhile, objects can be described using adjectives, and they can carry out different actions (methods). Let's take mathematical shapes as an example. Mathematical shapes can be described by the number of their edges, faces, and their type. We can have a rectangular shape, circular shape, triangular shape, and so on. This means that they all represent the properties of a shape in mathematics.

In short, objects have properties, and we can still associate events with the object. Object events are vital in programming. This is because they provide additional function and interaction between the user and the program. If you really want to know how important object events are, you need to imagine how a program may look if it doesn't have an event. It would really be difficult to achieve a lot of functions without events.

Now, let us review a few objects found in Excel. If you use Excel on a regular basis, you must be familiar with the following: Range objects, Worksheet objects, and Chart objects. Get ready to learn more about these Excel objects and how you can use them.

VBA Collection Objects

This is rather a straightforward thing because these objects are what the name suggests. Collection objects refer to the shape example which we used previously. We can use another example to illustrate it better.

36

Take a vehicle collection—we can have objects of type vehicle in different shapes, sizes, and colors. Rather than a single object, a collection provides the programmer an opportunity to work with objects found in a group.

The VBA language uses the plural form of the object type when referring to a collection of objects. For instance, Workbook object belongs to Workbooks collection object. This collection has all open Workbook objects. The figure below shows two Workbook objects (Book1 and Book3) and three Worksheet objects (Shee1, Sheet2, and Sheet 3).

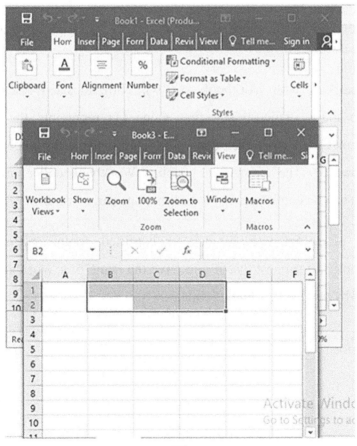

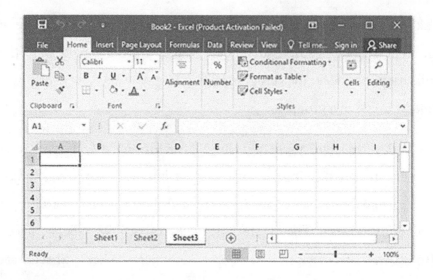

If you want to choose an object from the Workbook collection, use the code similar to the one shown below.

Workbooks(2). Activate

When working with Workbook, you will come to discover that there are two index choices. The first value (1) represents the current Workbook object while the other value represents the Workbook that is being created. The manner in which a Workbook collection object behaves can be confusing, but with time, one can come to master it.

But in order for you not to get confused when working with Workbook, we suggest that if you have the name of a Workbook, you select it by writing this line of code:

Workbooks(*Book2*). Activate

Object Browser

The IDE for VBA has a handy way to help one browse through all the existing objects in a project as well as look at the events, methods, and properties. This is referred to as the Object Browser. Use it to determine the Excel model and to know the objects available in the programs. You can also look at all the constants and procedures in the current project.

Select View —> Object Browser to open it, or you can just press F2. Before you begin to use the Object Browser, make sure that you load the library from where you need to look at the required object. Find the Object Model Chart if you wish for a graphical illustration of the Excel object model. But whether you choose to use the Object Model Chart or Object Browser, just remember that we have a hierarchy of objects which one must adhere to. It is essential to look at the object hierarchy as the path that will guide you to the object of interest.

Top-notch Excel Objects

Application object

This comes first in the Excel model. It represents the entire Excel application, and it is a unique object that rarely needs to be used in the code. However, there are a few cases when one may be required to use it: the OnTime () method, for instance, which is used in the program Math Game. Most of the time, you use the Application qualifier to declare features associated with the general appearance of the Excel window. You can view the screenshot below.

```
Application.Width = 600
Application.Height = 450
Application.DisplayFormulaBar = True
```

This object should further be applied together with the ScreenUpdating and WorksheetFunction features.

```
Application.ScreenUpdating = False
Range("A11") = Application.WorksheetFunction.Sum(Range("A1:A10"))
```

However, if you want to define properties of lower-level objects, there is no need to use the Application qualifier.

Workbook and Window Objects

Until this point, you have seen some of the Worksheets and Workbooks collection objects. You know some of the differences between collection objects and regular objects. Another important thing to note is that the Workbook objects rank higher than the Worksheet objects. Those who have used Excel before don't find anything new with this; you know that a single Excel Workbook has several Worksheets.

Not many people can be familiar with the Window objects. Window collection objects existing in the Excel application has all objects open. This includes copies of the Workbook object plus all Workbook objects. The indexing of Window objects is based on the layering.

Worksheet Object

We had previously introduced the Worksheet object, albeit briefly. This belongs to the Workbook object found in the hierarchy of Excel objects. The Worksheet object contains some events related to it. For instance, in a Worksheet's Object module, there exists an event procedure called SelectionChange (). A user entering a value in the current Worksheet would trigger this event.

The Range Object

This is a group of adjacent cells in the Excel Worksheet. In the hierarchy of Excel objects, it is located below the Worksheet object. However, this object is important because it helps one change the properties of a particular cell or a collection of cells in a Worksheet. When writing VBA programs, the range object will become very useful because you will need to use it in most of the Excel applications.

The Cells Property

This property displays a Range object that has one or more column and row indices in the active Worksheet. When you want to return cells back into a Worksheet, use the Cell property in the Worksheet and application objects.

Chapter 7

VBA UserForms and Controls

UserForms denote programmable containers that belong to the ActiveX controls. They allow one to create customized windows which can work as a user interface in the VBA application. They share similar features with VBA objects because they have methods, properties, and events. This chapter will help you understand how you can create UserForms with the help of ActiveX controls.

How to Design Forms in VBA

Those who already have some Visual Basic programming experience understand what UserForms are. For the benefit of the novices: this is basically a form. Since you may not have used VBA forms and this is your first time to interact with this concept, I want you to know that though you might see them as a Window, they aren't quite such. They don't come with a lot of features. For instance, you will not find maximize and minimize buttons. Furthermore, it has few properties and methods to allow one to modify the behavior and appearance of the UserForms object. But all that aside, these forms are still important when you want to improve the user interfaces of your applications.

Forms exist in VBA so that programmers can develop custom user interfaces using their Office applications. Thus far, the only way you know how to enter user data through the dialog box is through the two functions InputBox () and MsgBox (). It is possible to customize forms with the help of ActiveX controls, and it provides more ways for VBA programmers to collect user input.

Add a Form to an Object

If you have your project open and would like to add a form to it, you need to select UserForm from the Menu bar located in the editor. A new folder will show up labeled Forms.

Parts of the UserForm Object

Forms denote different entities in the VBA project. Additionally, each form has its own code that controls it. If you want to check the code related to the UserForm object, click on the icon called View Code from the Project Explorer. You can double-click the form as well or press F7. The general appearance of a code for a form is similar to other modules. In the upper-left corner, it has a dropdown list that has objects in the form. In the upper-right corner, you will find a drop-down list that has all event procedures related to different objects in the form. In addition, there exists a general declaration part used to create declarations of modules in the form.

The UserForm object contains different event procedures. This includes Activate (), Click (), QueryClose (), and many others. A few of these event procedures are common to other ActiveX controls. The figure below shows some of the most common ones.

```
SELECTED EVENT PROCEDURES OF THE USERFORM OBJECT

Event              Description
Activate()         Triggered when the UserForm is activated (i.e., shown).
Initialize()       Triggered when the UserForm is loaded.
QueryClose()       Triggered when the UserForm is closed or unloaded.
Terminate()        Triggered when the UserForm is closed or unloaded.
```

The Initialize () event becomes active when we load a form, and it's a wonderful location when the code initializes program controls and variables. The Activate () event is further applied in the initialization, but it is not activated when the UserForm object is loaded.

Adding ActiveX Controls into a Form

UserForm object, like the Worksheet object, resembles a holder that clasps other objects. When we add a form to a project, the Control Toolbox has to automatically show up. If it fails to show up, click View —> Toolbox from the Menu bar.

These form controls exist in a format similar to how they appear when added in a Worksheet. When it is placed in a form, you can access the ActiveX control properties through the Properties window. In addition, you can access the event procedures related to the ActiveX controls through the form module. If you would like to practice using ActiveX controls on forms, go ahead and insert a form to the project after opening your Excel. Modify the Caption property, as well as the properties of the UserForm object.

Show and Hide Forms

In Excel, you can display a form by triggering the Show () method. However, when you want to load a form without displaying it in the system memory, use the Load () method of VBA. You can then access all components of the UserForm programmatically once it is loaded in the memory. When you want to hide a form from the user but continue with the program control, the Hide () method is the best to apply. What this method does is to not clear the UserForm object from the system memory. Hence, through the programs, both the form and its details are accessible.

Modal Forms

The Show () method accepts a Boolean parameter which describes whether the form is modal or not. A modal form refers to the one which the user has to address, and it has to be closed before any other part of the Excel application can be accessed. When the form has no mode, the user can choose from any open Window located in the Excel application.

Unless there is a need for user interaction when the form is displayed, modal forms are secure. You can display the form through the Show () method from whichever place in the VBA program. But you must be aware that the way a program might run depends on the point in the procedure where the form has been shown.

Designing Custom Dialog Boxes

Generally, to collect the user input pertinent to the application currently running, forms are used as dialog boxes. The ActiveX controls help one to extend the function of forms from the basic InputBox () and MsgBox () functions.

Scrollbar Control

Most likely, you have used scrollbars in many applications to scroll through long documents. Sometimes, they appear automatically on the bottom or side of the VBA controls to help the user see the whole content. Situations like these don't need any addition; the scrollbars are present to help the user view the entire content. Still, in VBA, there are scrollbar controls which you can apply to the forms in your project to improve the interface. Other user form control includes the Frame control, List Box, and MultiPage Control and many others.

Chapter 8

Derived Data Types in VBA

In this chapter, we introduce derived data types in VBA, namely enumeration, and custom. The custom data types represent a vital data structure which permits one to deal with complex systems that reduce and simplify the code. Enumerated data types are not as complicated as custom data types. Instead, they have a simple data structure which creates codes that are readable.

VBA Custom Data Types

Having a single name, these data types are a collection of related elements of different types. An example is an application that stores and displays customer information found in a database. The database has related information such as age, address, identification number, and name. You may declare five different variables for each of these particular variables, but that would eventually prove to be cumbersome. In fact, the program would end up being longer and less efficient, not to mention difficult to read and difficult to write. Type and End type statements are used to define custom data types. You can see these below:

```
Public Type CustomerInfo
ID As Integer
Name As String * 30
Age As Integer
Gender As String * 1
Address As String * 50
End Type
```

In the example shown above, we have the name CustomerInfo given to a custom data type containing five elements. It is important to make sure that a custom data type definition is done in the general declaration module.

It is also essential that one differentiates between custom data type definition and variable declaration. The variable declaration describes the type of data but not the variable. This means that data is not shown by the custom data type. Therefore, it is okay to assign a public scope to the custom data type.

In the same way, you may want to declare an integer variable to your program's entirety, you may similarly wish to have variables of custom data type in the whole program.

Declaring a variable of type CustomerInfo is not different from a regular variable declaration. In the example below, the declaration results in the creation of a CustomerInfo variable called "customer."

```
Dim customer As CustomerInfo
```

To access individual elements of the custom data type, we use the dot (.) operator. This has been illustrated below:

```
customer.ID = 1234
customer.Name = "Fred Flintstone"
customer.Gender = "M"
customer.Age = 40
```

Other things that one can perform with custom data type include defining elements as arrays, declaring variable arrays, and passing elements of variables to procedures.

Enumerated Types

Enumerated types have several elements, and this data type originates from an integer data type. In this data type, every integer is assigned an identifier. The names of the enumerated types are constants. A constant will allow one to use symbols instead of numbers. This improves the readability of the program.

To define enumerated data types, it is a must to have its elements arranged between Enum and End Enum statements. Below is an example to demonstrate the definition of enumerated data types:

```
Public Enum Weekdays
Sunday = 1
Monday
Tuesday
Wednesday
Thursday
Friday
Saturday
End Enum
```

Within the Enum statement, all elements of an enumerated data type are assigned a constant value. The elements can have both positive and negative integers. When there is no exact initialization done, VBA automatically gives the first element the value 0, the other element the value 1, and so forth.

To declare the variables of an enumerated type, we have to use its name. We can assign them any integer value; however, there will be no point of having an enumerated type if we allocate the variable enumerate constant.

Chapter 9

Excel Charts

Charts represent an important tool to help anyone who wants to analyze data and present it in the Excel or spreadsheet application. The only obstacle to creating charts is that it takes longer and that it's steeper compared to other spreadsheet components. You will find this true when you want to program charts in Excel. One of the reasons that explain this difficulty is that the Chart object in Excel is a substantial component. Before you can start to program with the Excel's Chart object, we recommend that you get familiar with the common chart types together with their components.

The Chart Object

We use charts in the spreadsheet applications to interpret data. There are times when the analysis could involve a visual simple inspection of the numerical data that's been charted or even very advanced multidimensional curve.

Advanced data analysis comprises of looking for the parameter minima via the advanced space usually requiring a customized software hosted in a large computer. Thanks to the advancement in technology, this complex analysis can take place in any desktop computer that has Excel application.

When you are building an Excel chart, you can decide to connect the chart into an open Worksheet or a new Worksheet. Creating a chart and storing it in the new Worksheet would leave you with a new entity called a chart sheet. This is unique because its major function is to display the chart. You can't use it to store data.

In addition, the number of charts that can be embedded in a Worksheet is virtually limitless. When you want to use VBA to program chart sheets and embedded charts, you will need to know how to use different objects, and doing so may not be straightforward at first.

Chart Sheets

Earlier, we learned that a collection of Worksheet object belonged to the Worksheets collection objects. A chart sheet doesn't fall into this group because it is not a spreadsheet. However, chart sheets fall into two different object collections. The first is the sheets while the other one is the charts.

The sheets collection has a wide scope that includes chart objects and Worksheet objects. These are different to some extent because Worksheets and chart sheets are two different giants and a collection of objects stores only one category. However, VBA language has a collection of objects which hold only a single chart sheet. That is the Charts collection object.

It is essential to note that Charts collection object presented using a Charts property can only return chart sheets in a given Workbook. If you want to access a specific chart sheet, point out the index using the Charts property. In some cases, it can be difficult to apply the Chart property such that it would show a collection of chart sheets, including the charts that have been embedded in the Workbook itself. An embedded chart is the type of chart arranged on a Worksheet or chart sheet.

Embedded Charts

Accessing embedded charts would call for the application of both ChartObjects and the charts object collection. A ChartObjects collection object has all the ChartObjects in a chart sheet or Worksheet. It is a container which belongs to a distinct Chart object. As you can see, they may look confusing, but with time, you will come to distinguish between the two easily.

Manipulate Charts

There is a high chance that you have problems when it comes to accessing ChartObjects associated with chart sheets. In this section, we dig deep to see how charts can be manipulated, as well as discuss some of the methods one can use to do so.

Create Charts

If you write a VBA procedure which creates a chart, then it is important to make a decision whether you want to create a chart sheet or connect it to the existing Worksheet. The distinction between the two is very small.

Defining a Chart Sheet

The sub-procedure called AddChartSheet () generates a new chart sheet along with specific data from the user Worksheet that are arranged in a column. A dialog box highlights the range of the Worksheet that contains the data. The chart has Add () method, which is useful for creating a column chart in a new chart sheet.

Don't forget that Charts collection objects denote a set of chart sheets contained in a Workbook. Once we add the chart, the existing chart becomes active since it is the only element of the sheet.

Creating an Embedded Chart Sheet

For one to combine an embedded chart into a Worksheet, we have to apply the Add () method of the ChartObjects collection object. Then, we have the AddEmbeddedChart () sub procedure which helps one create a column chart as well as connect the chart to an existing Worksheet called Embedded Charts.

When you want to add an embedded chart, make sure that the Add () method has four parameters to set the position of the Worksheet chart. Don't define the properties of the Chart object if the chart does not have a single series object.

Chart Events

The Chart Object contains different events activated by various activities of the user. A few of these events are quite common, such as

Activate (), MouseUp (), and MouseDown (). However, we have some events which are special to the Chart object.

It is important to know that Chart events aren't automatically triggered with embedded charts even though it is possible to activate Chart objects for embedded charts. The figure below shows available chart events.

```
CHART OBJECT EVENTS

Event                  Trigger
Calculate              When new or changed data is charted
DragOver               When a range of cells is dragged over a chart
DragPlot               When a range of cells is dragged and dropped on a chart
Resize                 When the chart is resized
Select                 When a chart element is selected
SeriesChange           When the value of a charted data point changes
```

Chart Sheets

We enable Chart events using chart sheets. To record the events that are activated by the user in the chart sheet, take the event procedure that can be found in the chart sheet's module and create and combine a different code with it.

If you want to open the window that contains the code, follow the same steps you would apply for a Worksheet. However, it is essential to note that some events which are exclusive to the specific chart may not be applied somewhere else in the chart sheet because there is no means to activate the events. When data is present in a different Worksheet, it is not possible for the user to drag and drop different cell ranges across the chart. Despite that, the remaining chart events will continue to operate as expected.

Chapter 10

Error Handling

Nothing is as important as reading and writing data into the disk drives of the computer in most programming languages. In this chapter, we will look at some of the available tools in VBA which a programmer can use to write code and look at the various tools present in the VBA and Excel.

All computer programs written by developers and programmers contain errors. These errors are referred to as bugs. We say a syntax error has happened when a programmer goes against the rules of a language. The error could be a missing component in a code, a misspelled keyword, or an improper variable declaration. Such occurrences inhibit the program's execution, but it is not difficult to repair syntax errors.

There is another type of error called logic errors. These happen when the code has errors which might lead to the improper functioning of the program. However, logic errors don't cause the same results as syntax errors like preventing program execution. In fact, it's more difficult to spot logic errors. Despite all these, if a programmer abides by the rules of coding and implements correct debugging procedures, there would be limited errors in a program.

In addition to logic and syntax errors, a program's code can produce a runtime error which happens when a wrong input is entered. Some of the examples include the division by zero error or a missing file. Programmers are required to have an additional sense for errors such as this one because if they are not corrected, these errors will prevent a program from running. In short, the program will crash.

Additionally, these types of errors cannot be repaired by changing the program logic. In a situation like this, the program needs other means to handle the error found in the procedures. Whenever the program links with components of the computer and users, the error-handling code has to be present. Validation techniques are a good example of ways to handle error procedures.

The On Error Statement

This statement facilitates error handling in VBA programs. This error has to be followed with instructions for VBA to help set the course of action in case a runtime error happens. The action taken depends on the error type anticipated. This statement has to appear before the code that's expected to produce a runtime fault. The error statement is positioned close to the entry point of the procedure. In situations when an expected error needs the implementation of a unique code block, apply the GoTo statement of the On Error.

Chapter 11

Debugging

When you write programs, you will encounter a lot of problems and struggle to correct some of them. However, it is not easy to detect bugs in a program, and it can be frustrating and strenuous.

Break Mode

When a runtime error happens, a dialog box shows up with the option to click Debug. Once the Debug option has been selected and running, the IDE will also start, displaying the program in the Break Mode. The execution of the program when in this mode remains in the pause state, and one can go through the code line by line to identify factors such as the current values and the order of the code execution. In this mode, you will be able to see the line which generated the error.

If you want to enter Break Mode intentionally, it is important that you specify the points at the required points of the program using a Debug menu item. Breakpoints are also inserted at points where bugs are anticipated to occur when the program is running. This mode happens when the sequence of program execution jumps to the highlighted breakpoint. In this situation, you can choose to reset the program, scan through each line, and continue with the program's operation.

The value that is presently kept in the variable while in the Break Mode can be examined by hovering the pointer of the mouse near the variable name. Logic errors usually happen when a code allocates an incorrect value to a particular variable. With Break Mode, you can identify the errors which may have caused this problem.

There is yet another great debugging technique wherein you step through the code while it is in the Break Mode. You can press F8 if you want to run a single line of code at a time, beginning from the breakpoint. You can verify the execution sequence of the program as well as check the values stored in the variables when the execution of the code occurs line by line.

Immediate Window

Whenever you scan through a code line by line, it can be very stressful and tiresome if you can't get the error quickly. This window offers the ability for one to check program variables, as well as procedures in the standard program execution. To display the Immediate Window, press Ctrl + G when in the IDE. This window always holds a variable and statements to debug a program.

Watch Window

Apart from the Immediate Window, there is another important tool used in debugging VBA programs called the Watch Window. This Window allows one to monitor the value of a variable or expression in the program. While in the Debug menu, you can add Watch to a program expression or else right-click an expression and select the Add Watch option.

Select a specified procedure which you want to watch; it can even be all the procedures. The next thing to be done is to select a specific module that has an expression which you may want to watch, or else choose all the modules. Then, you can choose the type of Watch. This can be a break when we have a change in value. When the program goes into the Break Mode, the selected Watch type will appear in the Watch Window.

Locals Window

This window will show the variable values local to the procedure in the program execution. Make sure that you view this window before you move on to scanning the procedures in the code. This is an important tool when it comes to debugging, as it permits one to see the values of all variables that are local.

Chapter 12

File Input and Output

VBA language has a few objects, functions, and methods which one can use for file input and output. One example for file input and output is the Workbook object alongside its methods to save and open files. In this chapter, we shall discuss the most relevant tools in the VBA language that can be used to the aforementioned end.

When an application in the VBA needs a file I/O, it often requires a limited size of data stored in the variables of the program instead of the Worksheet. Excel gives you the freedom to copy data into a Worksheet so that you can save it in its general form.

File I/O

The Worksheet objects and Workbook have methods to help one open, close, and save an open Workbook in the same way a user can do the same tasks in an Excel application. It is possible to open and save Workbook files by applying different formats in the VBA code.

Opening and Saving Workbooks

The Open () method opens a Workbooks collection object in an Excel file. The figure below shows the syntax for the method, along with all the arguments.

```
Workbooks. Open(Filename, UpdateLinks, ReadOnly, Format, Password, WriteResPassword,
IgnoreReadOnlyRecommended, Origin, Delimiter, Editable, Notify, Converter, AddToMru,
Local, CorruptLoad)
```

It is important to note that you might not be able to use all these arguments. You can learn more about the terms you're unfamiliar with through online resources.

Use VBA File I/O

Besides the methods Open, Save, and SaveAs, there are other object libraries in VBA. Some of the objects are far too complex to be discussed in this chapter.

FileDialog Object

Existing in the Office library, this object is the regular dialog present in all Office applications. The dialog box allows one to precisely define the folder and files used in the program. This object has two methods. The first one is called Show () and the other one is Execute ().

```
DIALOG TYPES USED WITH THE FILE DIALOG OBJECT

Dialog              Type VBA Constant (FileDialogType)
Open                msoFileDialogOpen
Save                msoFileDialogSaveAs
File Picker         msoFileDialogFilePicker
Folder Picker       msoFileDialogFolderPicker
```

The Execute () method allows a user to define an action of the dialog box along with all the files in the Excel application. For instance, the Open dialog box provides the option for the user to select File and open the Execute () method in the FileDialog object.

FileSystem Object

This is an object collection method which you can use to define and extract information related to drives, files, and directories.

Open Statement

This statement is applied when reading and writing a data file. The Open statement has different arguments as well as a string which denotes a trail to a particular file. In case the file is not present, one is created. The open statement further needs an access mode and the number of the file.

Random Access Files

With these files, saving the entirety in the memory is not needed; one can simply access specific values within the file. This is achieved by ensuring that individual data elements have equal length before you can write the file.

Conclusion

We want to congratulate you for reading up to the last page. In this book, you have learned how you can create your first Excel Macro. In addition, we have helped you understand the VBA code behind macros. As you might have noticed, to set up an Excel Macro in the Excel recorder is not at all difficult. If your goal is to record a macro and play it, then you are now quite ready to go.

However, if your long-term goal is to become an expert in Excel Macros, it's my hope that this book has created the foundation and the right idea on how to record Excel macros and that it has given you a basic introduction to VBA programming. Besides that, I hope that this book has given you the confidence and motivation necessary to improve your Excel programming abilities.

Don't forget to look for advanced books to read so that you can continue with your journey of becoming an expert in both Excel Macros and VBA programming. Make sure that you immediately begin practicing macros creation, learn the VBA code behind each macro, and try other random things to see what results you get.

If you continue to read more materials and practice Visual Basic for Applications, soon you will be able to gain a better understanding of the whole process and create even more complex and interesting Excel macros.

www.ingramcontent.com/pod-product-compliance
Lightning Source LLC
Chambersburg PA
CBHW071553080326
40690CB00056B/1864